DATE			

ANN MORRIS

◆◆

LOVING

PHOTOGRAPHS BY KEN HEYMAN

LOTHROP, LEE & SHEPARD BOOKS
NEW YORK

First Edition   1 2 3 4 5 6 7 8 9 10

Library of Congress Cataloging in Publication Data was not available in time for publication of this book, but
can now be obtained from either the publisher or the Library of Congress.
ISBN 0-688-06340-3   ISBN 0-688-06341-1 (lib. bdg.)
LC Number: 90-33844

LOVING

Mommies and daddies
take care of you for a long time.

8

They give you food

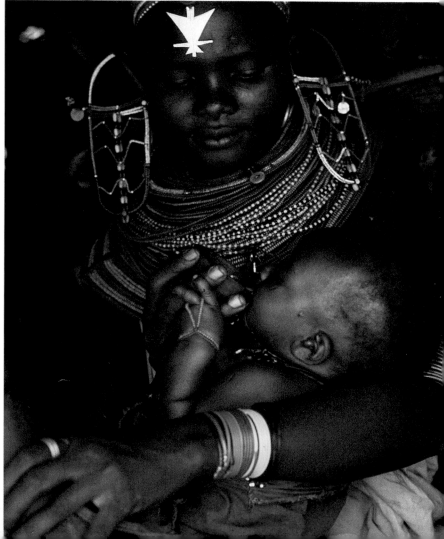

and keep you clean and tidy.

10   They make sure you are dressed and cozy.

They listen to what you have to say.
They tell you stories and tuck you in at bedtime. 11

They take you
to the market

and for walks
and talks.

14   They teach you to read

and to count... 15

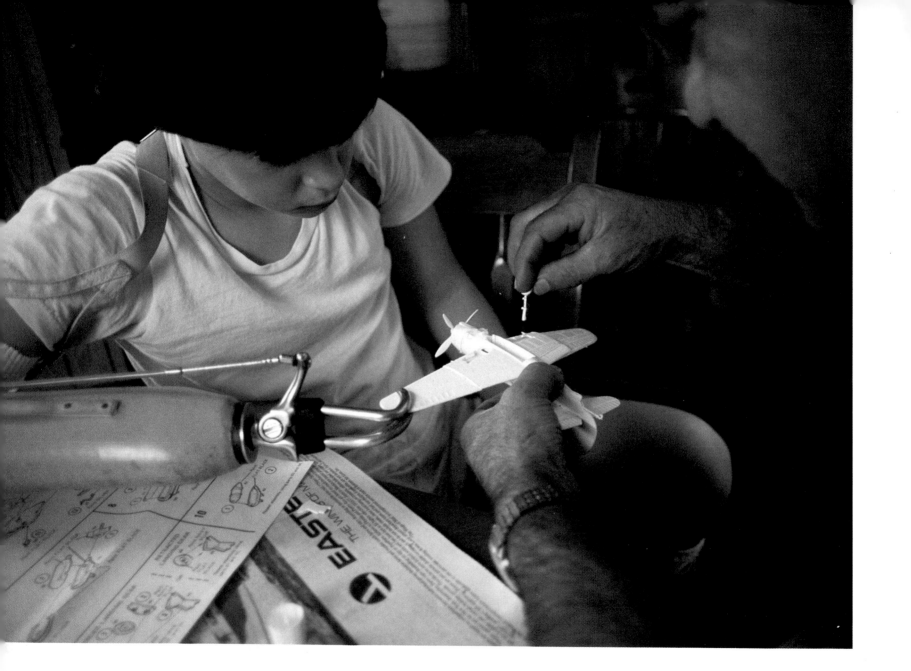

16   to build a plane…

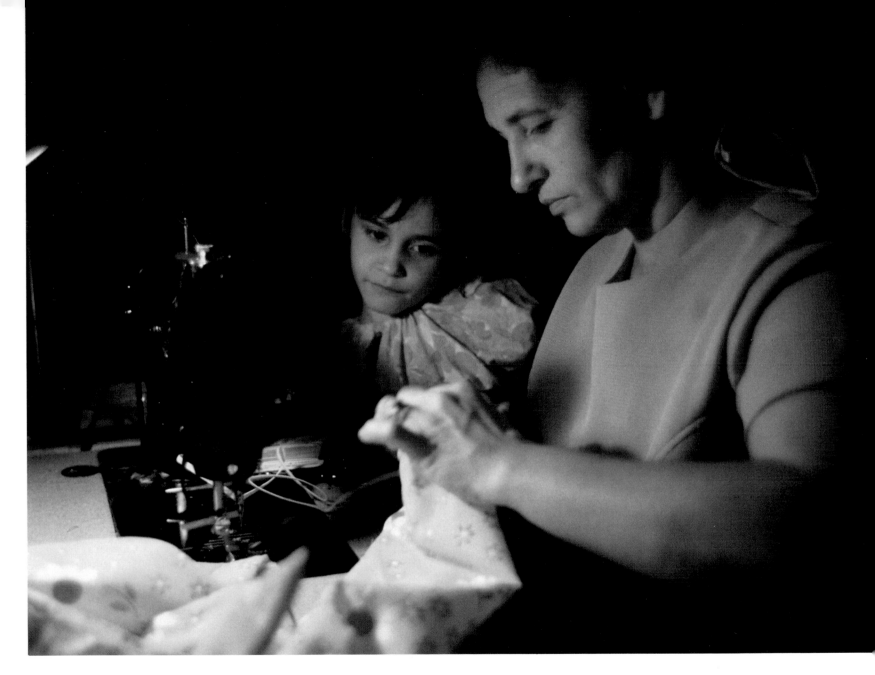

to sew. 17

18   They teach you how to ride a pony

and even how to ride an elephant! 19

They take you
on trips
to the city

20

and show you
the country
around you.

People who love you
tickle you and make you laugh.

They help you
when you're
feeling bad,
with hugs and
shoulders and laps.

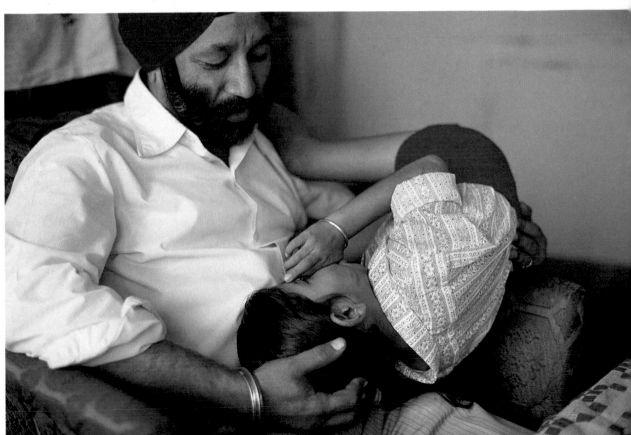

Older children
help younger children.

Good friends share good times together.   25

Children play with their pets

and care for them
in loving ways.

27

Daddies hug
and cuddle.

Even elephants
snuggle.

And mommies kiss and smile and open their arms.

INDEX

Half title UNITED STATES: This boy from the Appalachian Mountains has just played a tune on his father's banjo. His father is very proud of him.

Title page KENYA: The Samburu people are nomads who follow their herds of cattle to places where food is available.

5 INDIA: The red spot that the mother has painted on her forehead is called a *tika*.

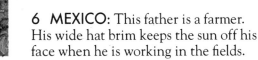

6 MEXICO: This father is a farmer. His wide hat brim keeps the sun off his face when he is working in the fields.

7 UNITED STATES: In San Francisco's Chinatown, many shops sell Chinese food.

8 UNITED STATES: This family lives in a section of New York City called Harlem.

8 KENYA: This Samburu woman feeds her child a mixture of milk and cow's blood. The mother's many beads are a sign of her wealth and position in the community.

9 UNITED STATES: There is no running water in this house, so the mother heats bathwater on the stove.

9 BALI: It's always warm where this boy lives, so he can have outdoor showers all year round.

10 UNITED STATES: This Navajo baby is in a cradle board. His mother will carry the cradle board on her back. The round piece protects the baby's head.

11 UNITED STATES: This boy lives on a ranch in Texas. He wants to be a cowboy when he grows up, just like his father.

12 UNITED STATES: This Afro-American family enjoys shopping together.

13 UNITED STATES: The boy and his father live at the edge of Monument Valley in Arizona.

14 ISRAEL: In this Orthodox Jewish family the father teaches his son how to read. Male Orthodox Jews must wear something on their heads at all times.

15 UNITED STATES: This Chinese-American child is learning to count on an abacus from her father. This is the way he learned to count when he went to school in China.

16 UNITED STATES: A mechanical arm helps this boy, who lost his real arm in an injury, build a plane with his father.

17 UNITED STATES: This Hispanic girl lives in Brooklyn, New York. Her mother sews at home to earn extra money for the family.

18 UNITED STATES: Learning to ride a pony is important to this Navajo boy. In addition to the pony, his family has four horses and two dozen sheep.

19 UNITED STATES: This little girl's family is part of a traveling circus.

20 UNITED STATES: This father and son are enjoying their day in New York City.

21 UNITED STATES: Ordinarily, this Navajo father wears his yellow bandana only on Sundays when he goes to tribal meetings.

22 UNITED STATES: Rolling in the autumn leaves is fun. This family lives in a suburb of Chicago.

23 UNITED STATES: Sometimes sharing is hard.

23 INDIA: This Sikh father is a photographer. You can tell he is a proper Sikh by his name (Singh), his beard, his turban, and the bracelet he wears on his wrist.

24 JAPAN: This little girl wears an obi, which is a kind of sash, around her kimono.

24 HONG KONG: The older child is a kind of child nurse. She has been taught how to take care of the younger children in her family while their parents are at work.

25 UNITED STATES: These boys are trying to catch catfish in a stream. They are using casting plugs to lure the fish.

26 UNITED STATES: This Navajo boy is sitting inside his hogan. A hogan is a round house with a center pole and a hole in the roof to let out smoke from a wood-burning fire.

27 UNITED STATES: These boys have a pet rabbit.

27 UNITED STATES: These children live in a trailer, which moves from place to place with the traveling circus.

28 UNITED STATES: The elephants are chained to a post so they won't wander off. They use their trunks the way people use their arms—for eating, picking things up, and for loving.

Where in the world were these photographs taken?

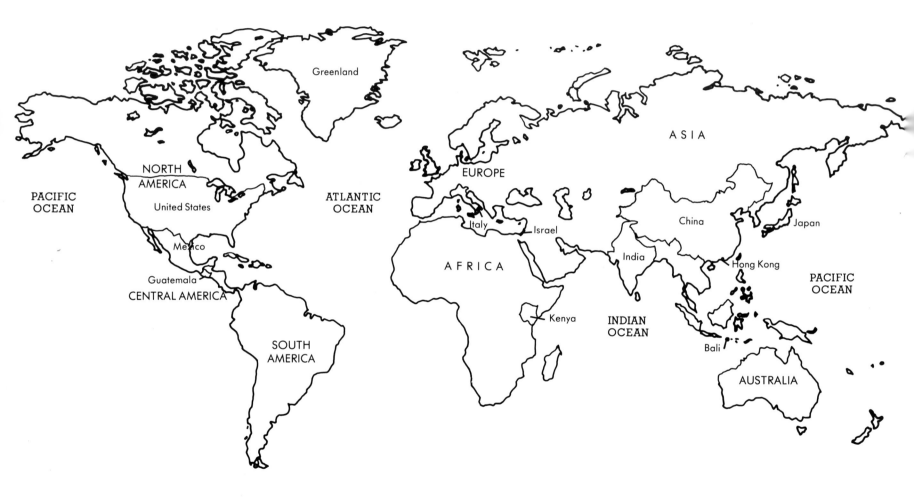